David Nockur

AF131034

A Character Analysis of John McIvor in Andrew McGahan's "The White Earth"

GRIN Publishing

GRIN - Your knowledge has value

Since its foundation in 1998, GRIN has specialized in publishing academic texts by students, college teachers and other academics as e-book and printed book. The website www.grin.com is an ideal platform for presenting term papers, final papers, scientific essays, dissertations and specialist books.

Visit us on the internet:

http://www.grin.com/

http://www.facebook.com/grincom

http://www.twitter.com/grin_com

John McIvor is a man of enormous drive and determination. It is the intimate bond with Kuran Station that propels his relentless strife throughout the novel, first to acquire it, then to keep it for himself. This paper will briefly outline the causes of this defining character trait of his and then discuss its consequences for John McIvor's personal relationships. Towards the end, the generational conflict that ensues between John and his daughter Ruth will be put into the context of the major themes of *The White Earth*.

It stands to reason that the vigor that he pursues his aim with stems from a deep seated psychological need, acquired during childhood and completely internalized by the time John reaches adulthood. Accordingly, in *The White Earth* the question of ownership is already raised in John's earliest childhood experiences.

Son to Daniel McIvor, who holds a managerial position in the Kuran hierarchy, John is bound for greater things. Daniel, a former policeman and, as we learn, "humble" of origin (p. 48), worked his way up and quickly rose through the ranks of the station personnel (p. 25-26). His own reputation somewhat stained (p. 48), Daniel's ambition concentrates on John, not only considering him his successor as station manager, but planning to elevate his son into the lofty heights of aristocracy, setting him on par with the ruling White family to finally claim the station as his own. This is to be accomplished through a marriage between John and the White family's youngest member, Elizabeth, the future inheritor of Kuran Station (p. 49):

> For young John McIvor, it was the greatest of expectations. His father never spoke of it directly, but the understanding was there, in Daniel's every look and word. Thus the seed was sown, and John grew up secretly believing that Kuran Station would one day be his. The thought filled him with pride, and as a boy he learnt every inch of the run, every corner and crest, from far out on the plains to high up in the hills. (p. 27)

Naturally, Daniel McIvor's schemes leave a mark on young John, who internalizes his father's ambitious plans. Daniel's implications are enough to instill in the young boy confidence in his supposed future, filling him with "pride" and anticipation. Despite the doubts that assail John from time to time, he cannot break with his plans. In the following excerpt, John, still very young, has to face for the first time that his expectations are not in tune with reality. Mirroring a later scene with his nephew William, John explores the object of his desire, Kuran Station, at the heart of which he finds a haughty young Elizabeth, well aware of the social barrier between the two:

1

And then, at the end of the hall, in the right-hand corner of the west wing, he came to one last open door. This room was all white and shone with an ethereal glow from arched windows hung with billowing gauze. *You shouldn't be up here,* she said. *Go away.* (…) And John went, his face burning, fleeing down the hall. How had she done that, frightened him so, when he was not afraid of anything? And how was it possible that they would be together one day when he couldn't even speak in her presence? But he had recovered by the time he ways back outside. She'd caught him off guard, nervous about breaking the rules, that was all. Their mutual destiny was many years off yet, there was plenty of time, and he would show her soon enough, when he was older (…) But the memory of that afternoon remained. And from then on, whenever he thought of Elizabeth, he would see her in that abstracted pose, framed by light, lost in her thoughts, and seemingly unaware that a boy named John McIvor, her husband to be, even existed. (p. 30-31)

The first thing apparent from the extract is the almost religious atmosphere in Elisabeth's room. The "ethereal glow" from the windows and the "billowing gauze" are suggestive of weightlessness. Together with the "white" of the room this creates a sense of divine detachment. All of this fits into the context of the scene. John's presence here is almost sacrilegious, he is not allowed inside Kuran House (p. 29) and class barriers separate him from Elisabeth. Also, Elisabeth seems to represent the highest of his expectations, she is, after all, the focal point of his father's lofty aspirations. And despite, maybe even because of, the obvious gulf between them, Elizabeth fascinates him. In this passage, John is obviously trying to overcome a nagging thought in the back of his head. Will the world concur with what he expects and demands? At this point, he can still reassure himself that it will all work out in the end, that there is "plenty of time" to "show her" his qualities. This assumption, however, will eventually also crumble. Essentially, the passage hints at John's struggle against objective reality, a conflict increasing in intensity with progression of the story. He is simply unwilling to to bow to the conditions of the real world and unable to acknowledge error in the face of defeat. It is this mindset that will later fuel John's zeal in the pursuit of his final goal.

When, in an unfortunate turn of events, Edward, the amenable patriarch of the White family, dies without leaving a male heir behind, legal responsibility for Kuran Station devolves to Elisabeth (p. 52). In a dramatic scene, Elisabeth turns on the McIvors, fires Daniel and makes it crystal clear that John, now a young man, will not be her husband. Additionally, Kuran Station will be sold out, with most of its farm land going to the government. John is left awestruck and impotent (p. 54-55). Being separated from Kuran Station, which has come to represent his destiny, deals John a crippling blow and puts him in a position that is unbearable to him:

> For John McIvor, banishment from Kuran Station was like an amputation. One moment he had been whole and young and full of hope. The next, a limb had been lopped away and the blood was draining out, leaving him cold and pinched. Elizabeth White had wielded an axe upon his life. (p. 71)

The above quote gives an impression of the significance the separation bears for John's future. Too rigidly has the expectation of ownership been established in his mind for him to abandon it now. It has become a part of himself that he is unwilling to let go of, an extension of himself, as the amputation metaphor suggests. What Elisabeth did leaves a mark on John, a wound that will not heal, that scars him for the rest of his life. It is this incisive moment that triggers John's later obsession. And with his "blood", his vitality, drained out of him, he will have to remain in a state of shock and depression for a while.

Robbed of his future and any orientation, John McIvor leads a desultory existence. He is a swagman for a while, leaving his drinking father behind, going from place to place without really having anywhere to go. Later, we find John working as a timber-getter in the Hoop mountains. These occupations serve him well as temporary distractions from the station.

Many years later, however, John is confronted with Kuran Station once more. His friend and future wife Harriet with him, he stumbles upon the station by mere accident and is immediately tantalized by the sight of it:

> It was one of the worst moments of John's life. (…) Visions of men and women dressed in white, strolling over green grass and reclining in shady recesses or by sparkling water, visions of a stern old man in a panelled office aglow with firelight, and, irresistibly, of a girl in white with curtains floating behind her. But with the visions came a terrible sense of dislocation – for how could any of it have happened in this barren place? It was all so dirty and shrunken and drab. John was hardly aware of Harriet at his side, peering through the windscreen. *What a pity,* she said, *it must have been a nice house once.* And an enormous throb of outrage swelled in him. A pity! It was far more than that. The dust, the blank windows, the front doors yawning emptily. He put the car in reverse and pulled away. Even that felt like desertion, as if the building was crying out to him for help. But what could he do? He steered back down the driveway, turned off towards the water

hole. But his despair only deepened as he drove. Everywhere he saw the same forlorn signs of neglect. Fences that leant or had fallen, piles of rubbish that had once been sheds and stables. When they came over the first hill, he saw that the little church too was sinking into ruin, the graveyard overgrown with grass. He didn't give a damn about the cemetery – let the Whites rot and their headstones tumble – but everything else cut with a pain that was almost physical. Bad enough that he had lost everything when it should have been his, worse still to find that no one else even wanted it! He drove the rest of the way in a furious silence, while Harriet gazed all unknowing out the window. (p. 144-145)

In this paragraph, we can see John's sense of entitlement to the Kuran property resurfacing. John's vision "of a girl in white with curtains floating behind her" is reminiscent of the earlier scene in Elisabeth White's bedroom. What is also becoming clear here is that John's obsession with Kuran Station has reached a point at which it is incomprehensible to the people around him, even those closest to him. The dilapidated state of the house cannot rouse Harriet to more than a fleeting "What a pity." when John is devastated by the sight. He, however, keeps his silence, signifying that he is unable to reveal his deepest motives to anybody. Instead, he shuts everybody out, creating a barrier between himself and others, one that later affects his personal relationships. Arguably, John's motivations cannot be understood by others, precisely because they are intrinsically egoistic.

His self-identification with the Kuran grounds evokes in him a feeling of responsibility for the deserted station, which seems to be "crying out to him for help". This feeling, of course, is rooted in his struggle against the perceived injustice of the world, that deprives him of what "should have been his". So this is again an instance of reality, in this case the property rights of others, interfering with John's sense of entitlement towards the station grounds. This is highly ironic if we consider John McIvor's later campaigning against native title legislation. It is the year 1993, many decades of hard work have passed and the station finally is in his possession. In front of a gathering of members of the "League", a political organization for the defense of the rights of land owners that he founded, John gives the following speech:

„[T]here's no turning back the clock. That's why I'm angry about this legislation. Not because of the Aborigines. But because the legislation is stupid. It ignores reality. It tries to make criminals out of honest people who have worked hard for their land, it tries to say that we stole this country, when in fact we earned it. The new laws will tie us up in a sentimental mishmash of impossible rules that pretend history never happened, that somehow we're back where we were two hundred years ago. We're not, and they are wrong." (p.212)

Here, John accuses those in favor of native title of trying to "tur[n] back the clock", "ignor[ing] reality", of "pretend[ing] history never happened". But what reason did the young John McIvor have to begrudge the Whites? Did they not, too, "work hard for their land" and "earn it"? Did Elizabeth not have every legal right to do what John so despised her for, to sell Kuran Station, a capacity inherent in a title of ownership. And what claim to it did he have back then other than "a sentimental mishmash" of impossibilities, giving way to a childish sense of belonging, a belief in fate and destiny?

His is, or rather was, a cause much more similar to the Aboriginal land rights movement than he can understand. Connecting them and an important theme in *The White Earth* is the inherent injustice that lurks behind the concept of ownership. This has to do with the fact that there are no objective measures when it comes to what is considered just. It is this injustice that the young John McIvor perceives when he decries what little attention the proprietors of Kuran Station pay to its ruinous state. Himself corrupted by egoism, however, a much older John will rather let Kuran House fall into ruin than allow the Heritage Trust to open it to the public, simply because he can (p. 225). Of course, John's notions of justice are rooted in his subjective needs. Failing to see this, he creates a double standard with regard to anyone else who is unhappy with the distribution of land, say members of the land rights movement. The aged John McIvor relies on, supposedly objective, legal definitions and egalitarian arguments to defend his right of ownership, e.g. his repeated affirmations that he "earned it" or his statements in the charter of the "League". Here, John uses classical liberal values like equality and "the rights of the individual" to back up his claim to Kuran Station (p. 133). But acquisitiveness, which we should think common to all humans, always depends on desire. He cannot see, of course, that his claim to the station was just as illegitimate in the eyes of the legal system when he first conceived it, albeit surely more egoistic and arbitrary, as the claims made by Aboriginal organizations are now.

John's ego-centrism gives way to another important conflict in *The White Earth*, the family feud of the McIvors. The scene which we will examine takes place at a time where John is doing better than ever financially. A few years have passed since John married Harriet and started off a farming business with the small fortune of her deceased father. Dudley, his old friend from his days in the Hoop mountains, has returned home from World War 2, mentally and physically exhausted. Himself a land owner, Dudley plans to leave all of his property to the couple when he dies. The following discussion between John and Harriet takes place after they discovered that Dudley was sexually abusing their firstborn daughter Ruth:

> He discussed the situation with Harriet that night. At first he spoke only of how Dudley needed their help, not the punishment of an institution. If they assisted him with cooking and cleaning, maybe he could survive at his own house? Harriet didn't agree. Dudley was beyond their help. The events of the previous night had proved it. He was becoming dangerous – not just to Ruth, but maybe to other people as well. Dudley, in his right mind, would never have wanted that. He needed professional care. Faced with this, John struggled internally for a moment, then came to a reluctant admission. It wasn't that simple, he said. And he outlined his concerns about Dudley's property. Harriet stared at him disbelieving. And so was revealed, finally, the immense gulf that lay between them. They debated far into the night. No matter how he tried, John was incapable of making Harriet appreciate what Dudley's farm might mean to their fortunes. In his extremity he revealed his hopes of reclaiming Kuran House one day, for all of them. *That old ruin?* She said, amazed. What did they want with a derelict mansion ten times bigger than they could ever need? And so John saw that his suspicion was right – Harriet was content where she was, and that far from wanting the House, she was repelled by it. And for her part, Harriet was appalled to discover what really lay at the core of her husband – a man so cold and calculating that his main concern wasn't for their daughter's safety, or even for Dudley's, but for property and money and a crumbling old homestead. (p. 223)

In the above paragraph, we find John struggling to make up excuses for keeping Dudley at their home. The other option, committing Dudley to an institution, John rejects, supposedly out of emotional attachment and concern for Dudley's well being. But he is only deceiving himself and Harriet. In fact, John has a stake in the matter. He needs to make sure that Dudley's will cannot be legally challenged, lest John lose the farm land that his old friend bequeathed to him. And at the heart of these considerations, of course, lies John's obsession with the station. For it is manifest that losing Dudley's land would frustrate "the careful plans John had made, the path he had laid out for himself and his family, leading all the way to the front door of Kuran House" (p. 222).

The passage (p. 223) is a powerful testament to the fact that John's preoccupation with Kuran Station is overshadowing the relationship with his family. As is apparent, he has difficulties discerning between his own needs, be they imagined or real, and those of his wife and daughter. He wants to procure Kuran Station "for all of them" and does not realize that "the old ruin" is of no concern to his wife. The inevitable rupture between him and his family, John could only avert by making pretenses and concealing his motives for many years. Harriet is "repelled" by the fact that the, essentially egoistic, pursuit of "property and money and a crumbling old homestead" is more important to John than his daughter's well-being. John's decision to send Ruth, against Harriet's will, to boarding school, keeping Dudley at home, (p. 224) epitomizes John's lack of accountability. Now that his intentions are out in the open, his preoccupation with rectifying the injustices that befell him can be seen conflicting with his duties and responsibilities as father and husband. Tragically and inevitably, the closer John comes to reclaiming Kuran Station, the more he alienates his wife and daughter.

The conflict is of singular importance for the progression of the story. An indirect result is that Harriet leaves John shortly after he buys back Kuran Station, unwilling to stay at the decaying old homestead, as we learn from a conversation between Ruth and William (p. 260). A more important consequence, however, concerns his daughter Ruth. Having cut all ties with her, over the incessant clamor of his wife and ostensibly because of a superficial quarrel about her choice of a husband, John abandons his earlier plans of making Ruth his heir and inheritor of Kuran Station (p. 270-271). With Harriet and Ruth gone, John McIvor finally relieves himself of all emotional bonds and human connections, his egotism coming to the fore:

> He was aware of a vast hollowness opening inside him, and all the pain and rage was falling into it, to vanish forever. He felt nothing at all, only an exquisite isolation. (p. 270)

There are other ramifications. Ruth, who saw being sent away to boarding school as a punishment (p. 224) and harbored feelings of resentment against her father ever since, is looking for payback. This certainly plays a part in her decision to help her mother divorce John, ruining him financially (p. 260). Ruth's thirst for revenge also features prominently in the resolution of the plot. Near the end of the story, John has finally found a suitable heir in William, in effect replacing his biological daughter, he and Ruth are having a heated discussion. It is revealed that Ruth has been making inquiries concerning the Aboriginal tribe that was based in Kuran Station at one time. Lawyer by profession, she has also uncovered the murder of a group of Aboriginal men, a crime that John's father, Daniel McIvor, bears responsibility for. The unclear legal status of the Kuran property and the fact of the murder, she contends, could give grounds for a native title claim, contrary to John's earlier assumption. Of course, Ruth does not root for her father:

> Ruth leaned forward. "I'll make *sure* they win. One day you're going to have to share this place with those people, whether you like it or not." (…) "You'd do it, too" the old man shouted, his last restraint giving way, a bony finger pointed. "you'd help them, just to get me. Anything, to steal what's mine. (...)" (p. 355)

The conversation between father and daughter, of which the above quote is only a small excerpt, makes it clear that the native title issue, in so far as it pertains to the station, has little to do with Aboriginal land rights. In fact, it is a very personal dispute. Poisoned by his greed, the relationship between John and his family has been reduced to a conflict about materialistic gain, which is money for one, and, first and foremost, Kuran Station. One example is the divorce. According to Ruth's later description, the separation from his wife troubles John much less than the prospect of having to cede half of the station to Harriet, which he can avert only by going into debt (p. 260). Similarly, the potential native title claim that is championed by Ruth is perceived by John as a threat to his property, another attempt of a hostile environment "to steal what's [his]". His daughter knows him well enough to realize that Kuran Station is his Achilles heel, deriving pleasure from the fact that she will "make *sure*" he will "have to share" it. She knows, of course, that to John this would mean being deprived of the station altogether. That this is about getting back at her father is acknowledged by Ruth at the very end of the story. At this point, John McIvor, in a desperate attempt to destroy the remains of the murdered Aborigines, has been tragically killed and the Station set aflame, hospitalizing William and killing his mother. John's will, according to which William was to inherit the Station, also perished in the flames. Meanwhile, native title has passed into law. Sitting in the waiting room of a hospital, Ruth reflects on the situation and ponders its possible consequences for Kuran Station, now that native title has been signed into law:

> Kuran Station belonged to no one. There would be trouble about that, of course. Her father had made his last wishes clear enough, but with nothing in writing, the property lay open to to any number of claims. Mrs Griffith, for instance. (...) Then there was

William. The station belonged to him now, if her father's last acts meant anything at all. But he was only a boy, and not her father's direct descendant. Ruth could dispute William's claim, if she wanted, and inherit the property herself. And perhaps she could really do it. But the thought roused no feelings in her, sitting there in the hospital room. When her father was alive it had seemed important that she … that she what? Take the station from him? But now he was gone, and all her arguments felt empty. She remembered, shamefully somehow, the old women she had met at Cherbourg, and the way they had watched her, as she talked eagerly of leases and land and rights. The look in their pale eyes. Measuring. And, despite all her promises, unconvinced. But couldn't she prove them wrong? If the property was rightfully hers, then why couldn't she give it away? She could go back to Cherbourg and hand over the deeds. But she was lawyer enough to know, perfectly well, that it would never happen that way. Mrs Griffith would fight it. Or maybe the boy. Or if not them, someone else. A long forgotten relation would appear; maybe even the state government would intervene, disputing the validity of private deals made decades ago, and leases that were supposedly perpetual … No, if anyone from Cherbourg really wanted the place, they would have to lodge their claim, along with everybody else. It was fifteen thousand acres of prime grazing country. In this world, something like that wasn't just given back. It had to be fought for. (p. 375)

This paragraph further elaborates on the conflict between Ruth and John and can be seen as hinting at its deeper meaning. Ruth admits to herself that her schemes were a way of avenging her father's lack of compassion, phrasing her acknowledgment as a question: "[I]t had seemed important that she … that she what? Take the station from him?" It could be argued that Ruth, a social progressive imbued with the spirit of the late 1960s (p. 266), represents a younger generation intent on reform. This becomes even more probable if we consider that the land rights movement started to gain in strength in the 1960s. That she is a government employee in the early 1990s, working for a watchdog organization focusing on right-wing extremism, might suggest that the belief system that she represents has become an institution in modern Australia, assimilated with it ideologically to some extent. John McIvor, on the other hand, a self-made land owner and founder of the "League", is the epitome of old Australia. The land-holding class that he stands for uses the pillars of western society to defend its property, revered values like the right of ownership, which cannot be easily challenged from within the system. This way, the antagonism between Ruth and John comes to represent a generational struggle.

If we take these assumptions to be true, then the paragraph above is a statement about social movements in general as well as the land rights movement specifically. That is, they gain their strength from the animosity of one generation towards another, the ideas they profess to represent serving as justifications for, rather than being the cause of, social upheaval. Losing their antagonist, as Ruth experiences in *The White Earth,* causes progressive movements to become somewhat disconnected from their struggle, leaving them without their revolutionary spirit. Accordingly, Ruth has to discover that "all her arguments felt empty" with the death of her father. This pessimistic account of social progressivism is also reflected in the opinions of those marginalized groups whose interests the movements supposedly represent. The remnants of the Aboriginal tribe that once inhabited Kuran Station, who never make an actual appearance in the story, secluded as they are at the Cherbourg reserve, are "unconvinced" by Ruth's promises to defend their rights.

This leads us back to the main theme of *The White Earth.* History is not governed by unanimously accepted standards of what is "right". Instead, it is driven by many different hidden agendas, all of which have in common only the fact that they are opposed to each other. This is a recurring characteristic in all generations and ages. Liberals like Ruth were unaware of this, of course, and believed that they were truly making progress on an ethical level, helping the disenfranchised, perhaps even becoming better humans in the end. And to some degree John had similar feelings with respect to the Whites. They inherited everything. John and his father had to work for it and knew the station better than the landed aristocracy. At one point early on in the story, John feels as if the station were "crying out to him for help" (p. 145). He tells himself that he would make a better owner, that he has earned the station, as opposed to the Whites who let everything fall into ruin. But none of these causes, taking better care of the station and giving back the land to its original owners, has intrinsic value. As has been shown, John and Ruth eventually abandon these goals because their real motivations do not concur with them. John, like the older generation he represents, claims to protect values like equity and equality when he really defends an outgrowth of his obsessive personality. And Ruth, representative of the younger generation, who seems genuinely committed to the Aboriginal cause, conducts a personal vendetta against her father.

To be sure, passing a law does not make the world a better place. Whatever progress has been made with regard to the land rights issue (Native Title Act), it was the result of irrational, emotional needs, the antagonism between one generation and another. By